femonomic
women "invite" crime

social issues and problems
in the poetic format

lovey chaudhary

Think Tank
Books

First published in 2019 by Think Tank Books
Website: thinktankbooks.com
Email: editorial@thinktankbooks.com
Lovey Chaudhary asserts the moral right to be identified as this book's author.

Cover by Gaurav Sharma

ISBN: 978-81-936204-7-2
Price: INR 299/-
Retail price listed is only for the Indian subcontinent.
Selling price may vary elsewhere.

to

all the good men out there.

about the author

A full-time poet, an unapologetic communicator, and part-time corporate slave to sustain her creative passions, Lovey Chaudhary breaks conventions through her writings. She's best known for writing about 500 articles on the subjects ranging from dismal societal order and how to get over the breakup and find someone better.

By typing "Femonomic" into Google, you can reach out to her. No, really, try it.

acknowledgements

This book is affectionately dedicated to my creator, my world; my *maa* and mother, with love. They won't read this though, so if someone doesn't tell them about it, they will never know.

To the one who contributed immensely in making me who I am, my main.

To Anita, who through thick and thin has been and remains a constant source of support and motivation. She also gave encouragement, often by asking: When the fuck are you going to finish your book?

A genuine appreciation to all the men who stood by women from the husband who drops his wife to the office to the man who puts the children to bed so the mother can have her own time, and to the friend who stands up for you when the bully thinks it's okay to harass women. Good men are becoming easier and easier to spot. It's been a long time coming, and we, as women are so happy to see it.

This book is dedicated to all those who emerged stronger and wiser even after the avalanche of life-shattering events.

And, I dedicate this book to you.
Well, you chose to pick it up and hold it in your tired arms.
Stay hydrated and look after your soul.

a note from the author

I'm not an expert on any of the social subjects I'm going to poetically address in this book. Although I have been an ardent observer of the societal order and its fandom for a long time now, still they shock me every day.

I've penned poetry on a number of social issues. Many of them, I truly believed in, but some of them, I wrote just because I thought it was something that should be addressed and written about.

We can say and do all the fancy shit about empowering women on Instagram, but it's no secret, the Indian society is known for its sexism, misogyny, and patriarchy. Women's rights issues are not always properly regulated in India, which can lead to several violations in the country. Despite constitutional equal rights, women regularly suffer discrimination million times a day.

India is the country where the birth of a newborn girl is mostly condemned and unsung. Even though women make up half of the country's population, many families prefer to be blessed with a male child than a girl.

India's literacy level is another major issue in India. It's even bigger in rural areas of the country, where over 63% of girls are dropouts because of well-known reasons to humankind. (Census 2011)

The crime against women is committed every 3 minutes, according to the stats held by the National Crime Records

Bureau. Women are raped every 29 minutes and every 77 minutes a dowry death occurs. The sharp rise in women (and men) related crimes is upsetting.

You can find people all around offering women free advice on how to live their lives, what to do, how not to get raped, how to cook and relentless how-tos and whatnots! Thanks, omniscient beings.

Ambition? What is that! Men are more important! Everyone can tell you that women are naturally wired to keep bottled up emotions for eternity and are therefore called more of the silent sufferers. Indian women are trapped in countless ways that they do not dare to engage in desires that otherwise, even in their psychic territory, come naturally to individuals.

The thing is you can't dare to expect acceptance from a society that doesn't even give a shit about the most fundamental grievances of women and simply loves to choke the very existence of women as per their obsolete norms and beliefs.

Do men feel safe from women on the streets? Do they choose when and where they are securely shopping or traveling without the fear of being groped or raped by women? Before parking, do men strategize, like not parking close to vans or trucks, because thug drunk women fool around at midnight?

Do men avoid going to the gym because their body will be objectified by women around working out? No.

Why can't women get the same? The recipients of unfair treatment in India are hundreds of millions of women.

Not everyone will be open to what we have to say. But battling injustice is a collective effort that takes time. Remember that doing nothing, changes nothing; speaking up always helps.

Also, before you dig in, activate your crude sense of humor and sarcasm.

Swami Vivekanand rightly said, 'Just as a bird cannot fly with just one wing, if the women are left behind, a nation cannot march forward.'

reasons for my writing

"Boys will be boys, they commit mistakes. It is impossible for 4 men to rape a woman."

- **Mulayam Singh Yadav**, Samajwadi Party Supremo

"If they don't want it to happen it will not happen. Those are the women we need to talk to and say *yaar* you need to change." - **Rani Mukherjee**

"Ants will swarm the place where sugar is."

- **Abu Azmi**, SP Leader

"If a girl wears jeans to her marriage, how many men will want to marry her?" - **Satyapal Singh**, BJP MP

"Objectifying women is completely cool that too on a public platform." - **Hardik Pandya**

"You ring the bell, I will bang you, Mallika." - **Akshay Kumar**

"This may be politically incorrect, but actually when I speak to a woman, I'd like her to be lying down." - **Shah Rukh Khan**

"How do people take you seriously at work when you wear lipstick and dresses and all?" - **A Bestselling Author**

"Rapes are an urban crime caused by westernisation, and do not happen in rural India rich with traditional values."

- **Mohan Bhagwat**, Chief of the Right-Wing RSS

"Don't protest. Hot sun will darken complexion."

- **Laxmikant Parsekar**

"Will ask my boys to go and rape CPM women."

- **Tapas Pal**, Trinamool Congress MP

"Rahul Gandhi's aide Meenakshi Natrajan, party MP from Mandsaur, is a *"sau tunch maal."*

- **Digvijaya Singh,** Congress General Secretary

"Two men raping a woman cannot be termed as gang rape."

- **K J George**

"The rising number of rape cases are connected to increasing population. Rape cases are on the rise in the country because men and women interact more freely now."

- **Mamata Banerjee**, West Bengal Chief Minister

"Virgin, as per the dictionary means, unmarried and pure girl."

- **Mangal Pandey**, Bihar Health Minister

"90% of the cases are consensual." - **Dharamvir Goyat**, Haryana Pradesh Congress Committee Member

"Every Hindu woman must produce at least 4 children to protect Hinduism." - **Sakshi Maharaj**, BJP MP

Now, don't most men believe that woman was created out of a man's rib?

imagine if things were different!

Honestly, being a woman is such an overwhelming task.

Come to think of it, Her mere existence can cause turbulence in the society; the uproar, the rape, the population boom, declining GDP. Basically, less Salt at the dinner table, and more monstrosities in the world!

She treats others as replaceable toys. Others endure exasperating experiences in her company. The blasphemous being plays around naked bodies without their consent. She strips naked from top to bottom and lays down her bosoms onto weaker sex; she is lustful, immoral and disgusting.

Depravity and discrimination are bred and brought up by Her in the world. She disturbs the worldly order by being born frantically & unreasonably.

Apparently, the degree of Her Loyalty is inversely proportional to the mortality rate in the nation. Acid attacks, marital rapes, and normalized disregard are a recurring phenomenon is her presence.

The fact that those strictly deprived of basic human rights are sublimated into wit and cunning facet of life by a mere woman is appalling.

Another interesting fact, men are only puppets a woman control and manipulate, so he is just titled 'sex', he has essentially been just a sexual being to Her.

For her, he is simply sex, absolute sex. Nothing more, nothing less.

She is always so "inflamed with the desire" at the mere sight of toys. I mean boys! How can She not when naked men are the most vital assets to the business of advertising?

She runs the world and greets tomorrow like it's fair and square. Male (male child) mostly is an unnecessary liability in a major way to Her. She carelessly hurls Sexist jibes and zillion taunts at men fighting for their rights.

Men are always so anxious about their fertility, Breath. Women don't want children all the time. Duh!

Open your eyes wide, sip a cup of coffee to keep yourself awake, and for the most part stand sort of tall like a tree when it gets thorny because I have just begun.

"girl child is a liability"

the fate of an unborn in womb

she is born
yet again her fate to be mourned
the crooked knife spills the bloody cynicism
she isn't worth a life

don't you have a heart
don't you care how she feels
what did she ever do to you
that you fed her a potion turned blue

her mother is not allowed to bear a girl child
even kept under the fear
unborn souls cry
whenever girl infanticide is tried

why the discrimination against them
when they only continue the generation
they only want to learn and write
and enjoy all the fundamental rights

she is proud to be a girl child
but your blood runs mild

infanticide

i arrived blindfolded into this world
to my little eyes the glittering light was too bright
i bid farewell to my dark home in her womb

i knew my future would bloom
from when i was inside her room
i lay on a cold night on the cold ground
besides my heaven was fast asleep

she would breathe softly in a heap
as i waited for her to wrap arms around me to embrace me
with her sweet love
profound hunger seized me making me feel gloved
but there were none around to nurse

like a good girl i was
i stayed quiet
but it just got worse
i saw a pair of hands coming toward me

the thirsty look of the father's sharp knife
eagerly waiting to end my dear life

"women invite crime"

his hairy bed

whose monkey is that
it appears to be having a quite chit chat
with freshly shaved pubes
that was once thick as a mat

i watch it rise without any grace
the man gives his monkey a shake
and behaves like she made a terrible mistake
being born a woman with round boobs for his sake

it is proud arrogant and overbearing
but has promises to crown for a sneaky break
tormented by hand jobs it never sleeps

it springs up from his hairy bed
with thoughts of violence in his dick head

a flash of rage against children and females spread
without a pause the monkey comes out
rapes ruthlessly and strips humanity into a mistake

reckless rapists

i was sinking into the sea of turbulence
more like an informal death sentence

did my choices carry me to hell in vengeance
i choked i gagged and i died
rapists only sighed when they were satisfied

i thought the soul had let go but i guess that wasn't true
because when the news broke out
only i was crucified

acid attack cycle

with her smile
she could brighten up a dull night
in a fully covered dress
she dazzled in the luminescence of light

she vanished out of sight
the moment a cynical man threw acid
to lazy her beautiful hazel green eyes

people probed
ah what did the girl do to *deserve*
acid in her eyes when she cried

too many women under constant scrutiny in the nation
but not enough humanity to go by

pedophiles

little children were just playing with toys
oblivious of chocolates handed by some grown up boys

after waking up to injuries
received by iron rods and cigarette burns in all kinds of holes

innocent souls discovered bare truths between childhood
and obscene

for regular readers of the news
it was yet another routine blues

slow death

i die regularly from the inside slowly
and all at once
i lied when i said “i am fine”

no longer is any of me genuine
i'm more scared to live than to die

my laughter is coated with scars
that i do not want to cure
looking happy is turning into a strain

nothing in my core but persistent pain
i was raped robbed and murdered over
and over again

the anxiety and depression combined
is a perpetual battle that numbs my mind

my joy has long since been hard to find
i want to destroy myself but never mind

murdered & set on fire

it was when her police complaint met with redundant
questions

she was left alone and traumatized to draw herself out of the
dump
the orthodox family brushed off rape as an accidental hump
she tried to forget
but grew tired after a time

she killed herself each day when she remembered
the terrible weakness in her arms at rapist's desire

beasts & where to find them?

when she resisted
she was unabashedly abused
deliberately drugged and repeatedly raped
tattered scrutinized and forgotten at last

the oblivious parents couldn't help but wonder
for how did the law and order
or judiciary let rapists so swiftly escape

how would they answer their grand-daughter
when she questions her own fate

dead upon the field of glory

in the warfare
fighting those they don't know
stabbing shooting and strangling
all without a hint of care

it's like a different day every day
for them there is no option to run away
one more sum of soldiers martyred
all dead and quartered as tv anchors inquire

the war with its deific smile
above mire dark and dense
leers manically serenely
is the sorrow of my own

my heart pains
for those whose suffering
is worse than mine

death stirs in the cold silent despair
while martyrdom reins the sky

women and balderdash

they say women behind veils are oppressed
red lipstick and chowmein are making them digress

scantily clad women invite crime and reverse progress
justifying rapes of children & women is charming
i guess

moral crusader's obsession with enslaving women
is something i couldn't care about less

i wish it was as easy as sending orbiter
lander and rover on the moon
but their only goal is to make women swoon
through violence abuse and rape on sandy dunes

to them women are always damsels in distress
dancing to the tunes men possess

sadly some think it's some kind of a success

when women are out

traveling in a public transport
is an ordeal of an everyday

it appears as if eve teasing is a man's right and privilege anyway
walking on pavements with lurking eyes all around is a story
for another day

no matter what you wear the less of a matter how you look
your body is in constant vigil inside or outside your sigil

they don't discriminate between dark or fair while harassing
eve teasing or raping
since the boobs butt
and the hole are all that matters

their honor
your honor
and all other kinds of honor rest only between her legs

how many more times must we say that it is not safe before it
is too late

it's not what she deserves
it's not what she wants
it's not what she wants to die fighting for
it's not what she wants to be famous for
woman life is not the one she chose
it's not what she signed up for

it is not about the girl or her clothes
it is only about you and how your perversion grows

you are responsible for the world we are living in
you are responsible for the path our future holds

you are responsible if something ever happens to your own children when the travesty unfolds

"terrorism balances overpopulation"

long distance love between india and pakistan

let me come alive let me step out and soar high
with you in my dreams
regardless of our country regimes

you seem distant or so it seems
the time difference is a rich & dark stream
but soon to my hope borders will be lush green

you don't know but then again
you have my heart in your hands
my love for you is on the mortgage of lands

cross the border soon and turn this house into a home

not being close to me is your only true crime
others in your life will come and chime
but my love for you beats the dime

i love you so much that my heart hurts
you light up my life but what about the questions in my heart

like can i kiss you as if it's my last

you are my sun
and the poem is almost done
i wish there was a remedy but there is none

so when you nap take this to your heart
that no borders can ever keep us apart

"women are like absorbent underwear."

tamed pet

i stood there naked gallantly
while it was snowing violently

i received red roses every day
then again seductions and quarrels
anger and grief were a regular play

again i learned what disrespect meant
in one winter dusk as my bruises swelled
and again a bell rang in my awry blood cells
and then again i was beaten bruised and battered

i wish i knew his reason why
my eyes were forcibly shut
then and thereby

"men women maketh each other"

tender gender

i may seem tender but you can't possess me with your vile and vicious slander
for you i am no longer an easy surrender

journey to teenage to adulthood

back then i knew myself as a woman none could ease

later i was hypnotized
by your brown colored eyes

those holding my gaze
outshine your well embellished lies

with you it has been a roller coaster ride
because this lust of mine
convinced me the rust in you is fine

you make me alive
you make me despise
you make me fly
you make me die

so now let's just say goodbye
and simplify the swings
between you and me

noxious masculinity

they conditioned me to think
i exist to please and wink

they believed puberty made me drink
and my boobs could never sag or shrink

in all its glory and splendor
tremulous and tender
the chauvinism since the beginning
was an easy offender

but then again i am going to emerge stronger
for the ones who fought and the ones who remain
because dayum noxious masculinity calls

stand your ground

a society dead or alive
dictate women whether of five or seventy-five

to me it doesn't even come as a surprise
with no will to living life is all over again a fight

don't get paranoid and be delusional
none will stand up
for your fickle and fleeting rights

fight for your rights even if everything else bites
die for what you think is right even when the tide is high

feelings are like a delicate flower

i was gentle tame and meek
but now barren i don't speak

choose your battles wisely
since even a *"delicate flower"* can shatter egos
and kill so kindly

let me help you with your broken pieces
also remember charge cess
when you gift your feelings in a package

merry marriage

we shared a life together
smelled flowers every day
and were closer than ever

you were like oxygen in the air
but the way we lived crumbled
while i was unaware

you stranded me alone with throbbing nightmares
the choice was yours
you chose your quest

i got dressed
chose the best
and built a beautiful nest

marriage mask

the marriage is such an imperfect buy
setup on jumbled laws of demand and supply

some may defy
the bars to meet upon a common ground so high

everyday questions of what should we cook
hot pie

jumping to your own conclusions
building a concrete wall of constant confusion

living a life full of illusion
glancing back lying on made-up delusions

exes

well honey
i've got some news for you
your designer clothes are now in rags

i've got my shit together
and i am in control

hey man
breaking news
you're just a big asshole

you
a degenerate soul

***"bad things happen in a society.
get used to it."***

crime & punishment

one of many tainted times
the crime is not rewarded
with the retribution along the same lines

the archetypal excuses of the judiciary
and typical society
are silently soaked in sanguine saccharine
grinning gingerly
about legal implications and sentence

how ailing it is
for you to drink
three cups of justice and two lattes of equality
to hydrate pages with some ink while righteousness await

mental malice

the crumbling human fabric
the stigmas from horror to comics
weave regular causalities with or without guns

they call it impiety
i say the lack of propriety

the acumen of caste gender race or colour
be it exploitation illiteracy & hunger
more so infanticide rape afore domestic violence
to name a few poverty waltz like motion in silence

the earthy mental malice
has even mr. almighty puzzled
just imagine no bombs no more violence
but the sound of joyful silence

let's raise our voice with confidence
whenever in the presence of tyrants

the rat race

what the fuck are we doing
holding spear in our hands and brewing
vivid wild dreams and losing our minds

they are testing bombs
they are dropping bombs
they are building even more bombs
they are sculpting lit & warped drones
with carnivorous forks and horns

are we really killing shooting and bombing
over some religious writing
we are trying to de democratize the democracy
because of rumored magical cup hypocrisy

still
what the fuck
why are we killing several hopes & dreams

cease and deceit

how many hearts will die
due to the web full of lies

how many of us will suffer
before the nemesis steals our treasure

i hear them pleading for kindness
i see them searching for love
i see children crying for a living

how many of us will turn into martyrs
in this world full of chaos and anarchy
how many of us will survive the web of lies

ragged children

such is the irony of fate
all free and frayed
but can't be kindled with desires

for choices were made
the time they were born poor
resolutions were made to rob them of their rights

and it makes me think every time
do they dream who sleep on the pavement
they smile they laugh
well aware of the joys they can't have

just another human after all
epitaph so simple for them to live by
kindness & empathy feed hearts when flames aspire
hopes to see them soar higher unto skies of fire

prostitution

i wish to absolve aching
i wish to stall shaking
i wish to block breaking
believe me i'm trying

but then again i wish my heart just
stops beating
as i dwindle down into moneymaking

maybe i will recognize it someday somehow
i’m more than just a plaything
i’m more than my self-depriving crimes
done in the past times

it can bungle me sometimes
even i can grow a spine
or it’s just another fleeting thought in the back of mind

hypocrite

the world is big and tall
an inescapable cage
full of hypocrites and surplus rage
it is not getting any easier to engage in this age

"can the damage be undone for what our world has become?"

infinite sleep

you know i could sleep till eternity
if i didn't have to wake up to eat pee and beep

my mind doesn't wander when i sleep
and that is exactly why i dive deep in sleep

if you are anxious
sleep baby sleep

it is so sweet and cheap

the phone

we are looking at our phones like a clown
that is why our mothers hammer us down
to them it is the cause of losing our crown

but i want you to be happy
wandering albatross in your kitchen gladly
munching on pizza or hamburger madly
wearing shorts clicking pout selfies on your phone proudly

from my corporate to yours

i am so bored to death at work
aren't we all just some
random corporate jerks

i totally think my boss is
just another clerk

i am left with nothing but
a bigger butt

i retain diplomacy and
count days backward
to timely receive my pay check

musings

poetry without rhyme
for me is an amusing pass time
for me who aborted literature mime

some swear by the money
some swear by the thrills

i really couldn't care
for these fancy limo and frills
while they run the worldly ills
i and my friend calmly chills

plastic planet

unforgivable
is what we have done to our planet

plastic is ubiquitous
from arctic to antarctica

the cause of death of sea turtles and choking of whales
is hills of 18bn plastic in the world oceans

the frequent use of
single use plastic has us literally breathing microplastics

one day
mass of plastic will exceed
the mass of fishes if we don't stop now

pledge for a #plasticfreejuly and be fantastic
because it kills more than just humans
and death by plastic is drastic

they are all the same

the seekers of knowledge
the believers of cosmos
the saints and wildlings
are all the same if they are given a chance
to commit sins and loosen up belt loop of their pants
into the vast expanse of crimes

bitch or what

do they think
bitch
dumb slut
witch and words alike
can make women twitch

it is just their own benevolent itch
that manhood and its magnanimous ego
can only become rich
by calling woman a bitch
sitting amongst its niche

get over your pitch that
she is only here to reproduce
as her resistance is of no use
just know there will be revolts if all hell breaks loose

the tragedy of self-love

i don't know
how to capture the essence of 'self-love'
and pour it out there

all i know is you are greater than your fears
phobias and hurt
you are enough
more than enough
even when the winds are rough
you are the solution to all your sufferings
you only can offer you the courtesy of whirring wings

i've said it once
i've said it twice
and i'll say it another million times

love yourself deeper
softer and kinder

because you are truly yours carry it as a reminder
you are not anyone's spare crap
it is as simple as it gets
don't choose the lesser life

live yours and truly yours
that pumps your lungs
that drips from your sweat
that sees you right in your eye
that seduces your greater self

sane

i don't have to be pure and pious
for your sake
i am way more than just a beautiful chaos

why is there so much unnecessary noise
i don't like superfluous joys

don't let your demons be louder than the trains
darker than the dark
bluer than the sky
and friendlier than the family

for your own sanity

"self-love is selfish."

never mind

if you feel you can't do it
do it
if you think you can do it
do it even better
because why not ameliorate
never mind
or you can just sleep and escape

break it down

i have always wanted to break down ceaselessly
i have always wanted to give up unknowingly
i have always wanted to be held softly and told
it is okay to take time for days weeks and months
and yes one at a time

i was always scared to live through the stormiest days
the occasional appearance of my intense fears & night terrors
frequently brought catastrophe
with an aching impulse to escape

they called me irrational and crazy
i don't blame them

they understood me but to the contrary
i urge you to take action before it's too late
because you are responsible for thy state
you only have the key to unlock the anxiety gate

societal insecurities

no
that wasn't the deal
i signed up for when i was born

i didn't deserve their scorn
they opposed my existence till i was reborn

it's not that i didn't believe them
it's just that i didn't care
i never gave up

i was already high on the peak of a lush green mountain
before they showed me the bottom my place

it was finally time to let them go
and for me to finally grow

anxiety at arm's length

wish i had let myself breathe
when anxiety choked me to wrath

wish i had let myself live
let go and forgive
had i known my power years ago

so was the need of the hour
now that i am dead
i laugh at love and care

i look out the hell to begin the day
the sermons of self-love as anxiety beside me silently lay

who am i

i don't know why i cry when i'm angry

i don't know why i fight when i'm sad

i don't know why i lie when the truth will do

i don't know why i eat shit when i can do keto

i don't know why i laugh when in pain

i don't know why i giggle silently when i'm glad

i don't know why i'm silent when scared

i don't know why i speak when i'm unsure

i think i'm emotionally irrational

and viscerally in charge of my emotional expression

unfair

i didn’t expect life to be fair
as it is unfair to everyone
so that’s fair i guess

i can't tie up my hair anymore
because i cut them in hopes
that does away with dead ends
will fill me with light again

nothing gets me down

i cry in non-compliance
i try harder in defiance

not a day passes by when they tell me i am not self reliant
sadly it's sad to see and hear everyone behaving like a giant

the trees drop their leaves
birds no longer sing the songs
i gasp for breath on every mile i am wrong

but i get up and battle the day
i've come so far that nothing gets me down anymore

i am ready to spread out
my waddling wings that nobody can ignore

fearlessness

i'm trying my hardest to be okay
a song has the power to reduce me to ashes
i wish i loved myself more

i'm trying my hardest to be okay
but a couple words in the wrong tone
can still make me breakdown for hours under the shower

i'm trying my hardest to be okay
but i can't bear to be alive sometimes
it pains so much that i can't sleep

i'm trying my hardest to be okay
but a negative thought can wipe away my strength

i am all alone
i'm trying my hardest to be okay
but i can't stop crying
but i can't stop cutting
but i can't stop hurting

yet i will get better
and that's all that matters

tell me

tell me how to stop eating chocolate at night
with no hopes and dreams

when i feel like drowning in despair
tell me how to fly with no wings in no wind

every time i rise up
i just fall
now i can't stop eating
the chocolate cake

it feels like my eyes are shutting
i consistently feel my senses slowing

don't stop eating chocolate now
gotta keep life going

"self-satire"

i don't know what to name it!

can we ever know who we are
are we not different every morning and night

isn't it dependent on the state of mind that you experience

to be happy all the time can be pretty pleasing

but what about the anxiety anger and frustration streaming inside

stay hydrated and look after your soul
you got only one
therefore strive for nothing less and be a whole

a war with myself

i have cut my skin
around the wrist so thin

an ache to revoke the torment
made up for lost time with myself

i moved toward becoming devoured
by the extent of my own desires

i can no longer escape my pain
now that the laughter will never show up again

lived a full life despite

she arrived with some booze
laughing out loud
reaching for the keys in her pouch
entered the house and buried herself on the couch

she took off her clothes & shoes
to lie down leisurely on the sofa
only to realize she had not paid her dues

that day she lost all her relationships
family
two of her best friends and a long term partnership
she looked at the ceiling with wide eyes open all night
she was blank the whole time and seemed far from alright

she felt nothing
nothing at all
but she never stopped fighting for her life

living it

i recently realized things don’t get better
if you run away

you can't experience a sigh of relief in a carcass
you can’t run from your own shadow
since you can only see darkness with dead eyes

presence

i keep seeking answers to quench my thirst
all i receive is a hush that kills nothing but time

i have heard silence speaks louder than words
i don't know if that works

of course it has its own perks
since i can't defeat the silence in its turf

death

i always marveled at how dying feels like
do you ever too

let me know if you figure out before me
my wandering soul will find you

i now understand death is not the end
the beating, the bruises and constant sadness are my real friend

night

there is no light inside you
it's a dark and a dwindling deep web of darkness

your soul is the same colour as the coal
darkness is all the things beautiful

it is your true friend
it is silence solitude and peace

flashback

i only visit my past
i don't live it
past is a mere cast
past is a waste paper
past is the last used toilet paper
done and dusted
it will rejuvenate your mental health
if you forget it fast

tumble

i am not your jill you are not my jack
you are alone fighting an uphill task

i am telling you
you are going to blast

i am not coming with you
because i know it's never going to last

leave me

i am so exhausted at times
i want you to leave

let me go
and let me be on my own

without you
the seeds of growth will be sown

without you
i will go out & explore the unknown

bespatter

i said
you make my world better

he replied oh that's another matter
and ruined the friendship built anew

i grew a spine stronger just in time
after his ruthless bespatter

paycheck to paycheck

the career is a constant struggle
day to day life is more than just a bubble

the paycheck to paycheck living is a burden
eyes meet expectations with no curtains

my soul screams louder than i am hurting
it is certain that everyone was just flirting

putting me in my place
by jerking off to my face

i had had enough lessons by god's grace
but the ways of life had me in the rat race

"love"

twelve o'clock truths

i fell in love with
the con version of you

i fell in love with the beating
bruises and your constant retreating

i kept pouring
yet your love was never reassuring

you are an addict
but i am not your rehab

mind you
i am just a visitor
my journey is more of an executioner

to love

to love
and to be loved
is like a whirlpool

listen for a second now
that i got you double checking
catch your breath
be brave and try to keep cool

love is warm
unpredictable and most foul
it is going to hit you hard like a wrecking ball
when you lend it your all

self-centered

i whisper my dreams and nightmares
to your guilt laden affairs
while you imprint your fingers onto my lips
like the splendid silence of an eclipse

in the face of your profound pleas
i melted onto your knees
only to be left alone drowning in the ocean of sorrow to freeze

concealer

love makes all our pains go away and the world go round
it also makes you fatter and flatter like you matter

the thighs under silk sheets get wilder & madder
the hangover wears off soon
when they wake up to a new platter

go ahead love
just wanted to say
love is a rotten batter

the crux of the matter is love works as a concealer
and red lipstick
acts even better as a healer

relationships

relationships are hard
you can't be attached hip to hip
even though it is forever a sinking ship

straight or same sex love
is a weed out dead wood

first
the social struggle to be labeled as a couple
then to maintain the status quo even after rumbling troubles

toxic relationship

bleeding from the jaded veins
once afresh your leftover tshirt remains

you still are the reason for my being
yet your faults loom beyond my foreseeing

you are my passion and you are my pain

your abandonment makes me cry
the broken trust makes my heart rift
i don't know why

i believed i knew you
now we are all set to get ugly and how

i want to shred you into pieces
and let you cry for some mercy

but then again i am writing this while
wearing your old jersey at twenty nine

imbecile love

i'm fighting this writing
i feel more like i am drowning
trying to catch my breath
while my heart is pounding

i can't explain to you
imagine a person
just like you
living parallel to you
singing your songs
early in the mornings

i'll be honest it still scares me
our energies connect
means we are together in universal respect

before we were this
we were something far away
attached to the rhythm
of our own night & day

my desire as the sun
your patience as the moon
so closely attuned like water

you've let me peer into your darkness
as you have somewhat seen into mine

but even in those moments
i see you in me
i see me in you
nearly extinguished
flame diminished
in exquisite darkness

i love you more than you will ever know
is this forever
i don't know

right now
i just need your hand in mine to show

consummation

she always wondered why he even tries
despite the lies spoken at night time

at first he consumed her
her fragile soul
i don't interfere but to each their own

the seeds of love had already sown
i guess she never learned
that's why she crashed and burned

it was too late to save her soul
he had lost control
confused with lust pride
and greed

he had created a mess
with the demons that roamed his filthy head

feelings & reality

he says
i love you
she makes faces and never says it back

maybe to say it back will cause meteorites
to fall back upon the earth

when he kisses her
she coldly leans backward in detachment

still he falls madly in love
with her in no time

she died from a hole in the heart

just before the day
he planned to propose

he silently learned to wither
and slowly die

bed with red blood

the bed feels oddly new to me
it's a broad island of memories
i can now lay my arch down let go and cry

i carve my failing heart on the bed in your favorite spot
the mess full of silk pillows is still etched with your face
so is your smell that never fades

take the sheets in which we made up after fights
i can't anymore look in your brown big eyes
i can't watch you boarding the flight to leave

i'm just stranded on our isle lonely
i can never fall in love with anyone but you
you were and are my one and only

i absolutely think we are together in the parallel world
i'll love you for as long as i can

i am on our bed which is red with your thick crimson blood

the ex hurts like the wax

we meet again
in order to chill
to unleash more of our thrills

deep within
i knew it was only about her skin
i am more than sure
it wasn't a shameful sin

to enjoy the melancholy of her hair
more despair but her eyes full of tender care
i watched her hum

she drew animals
mammals and running rabbits on my back
i took a moment to appreciate
her moans
her questions and her hate

i would do it all over again
be it in thunder lightning or rain
i fade away and devastate while
she still celebrates hate & pain

love

love feels like a different wonderland each time
there's something magical when it's at its prime
but why does it feel like the crime so sublime

love feels right in sight each time
daydream weddings begin with might

as it travels across your tender heart ceaselessly

with its exquisite painful wings
this lovely torturing love
sirens so hauntingly
upon approach

we might somehow riff
as bittersweet requiem kills my yearning soul with pleasure

this love
a lilting candlelight treasure
softer than a cloud caressing herself

until a new lover comes along
and you turn into another memory on the shelf

i wake up to you

when i wake up in the morning
you're the first thing on my mind

no matter the date
no matter the time
you're the one for me

can it be true
is this true love i've found

i have been in love before
but nothing compares to this

you've touched my heart and soul
you run on my mind all day & night along
in places others always missed

you are so captivating and comforting
this love feels so complete on repeat
and oh your stolen kisses are scintillatingly sweet

your lips are mine

i loved your luscious lips when they used to be wet with mine
and how they left a territorial stain

i am not sure if you know
but your arms now choke me to death all the time

you used to love my dark damp hair in the mornings we met
your wild kisses were the best against my flesh
you can't kiss me anymore sweetie with your warm wet mouth

and say with a passion born out of the youth
that my body and soul is yours in truth
the house is called yours not mine

i am like that leaf in fall
that is finally going to say bye

dreams

spend all your life with me
you set my poor heart on fire

clasp me close in your arms
till the shining stars are alarmed

let's wobble our wings
and fly away today
faster than the speed of light ray

meaning to love

there's more meaning to the word "love"
it's not the simplest to explain
there are many mixed feelings

none of the same

love to some means happiness
to others it brings tears
once you've fallen into it
you're stuck with it for eternity

there's no escaping love with ease
for it takes quite some time

some never find the exit out
for their love is called blind
not realizing his love for me
would suddenly just wither and die
advice #543219
never let anyone else become the reason you wake up in the morning.

you will make a total fool of yourself
just a warning

to a dark moses

you make me feel much lighter
i think this time
i had taken a hit

you look smitten with love
you are what i seek
i wonder where you were last week

i have never kissed lips gloomier than yours

i can ride on yours for like hours
and i promise you will shriek
i have never seen eyelashes longer than yours
you tell me my face looks adorable when i am on all fours

i am burning with passion
let me devour you in a few more sessions

infectious love

this love is so infectious
that i can't get away from

it is like a disease
that takes control of my body
this love seems impossible

i am not able to take it back
it's already a fraction of my life

this love is perfect the way it is
my life would not glean the same minus it

just remember how everything began
it started with a hello
with words that were never spoken
feelings that were hidden in the ocean deep
only you i wanted to see

it started with just one hello
now my heart won't let you go
the blissful face i see in you
can't get out of my head with a single blow

i heard a sound deep within me
calling your name in a special way
my heart started to race on that day
can't understand what it wanted to say

how can i tell it to you now
even your shadow i can't find somehow
i can't wait the day after tomorrow
to say to you these words i really like you

i want you to hear my solemn vow
came deep inside my heart so listen carefully now

this is the right time to let you know
words like i love you are purely true
i want you to look into my eyes
to let you know the naked truth and lies

someone like you was on my wish list
in my dreams there is you and me
day after day it's still you that i see
if that sweet dreams will turn into reality
understand that my love can last until eternity

erotica on paper

i made love to him on paper
and spilled ink like passion across the notebook later

i caressed his hair in every love letter
i kissed up and down his thighs in short sentences and prose

i tasted all his innocence without a spoken word
i bit his lower lip and pulled his hair in between the lines

i made him arch his back moan and scream
surprisingly
it only took me a pen

play with me

lay down or you will drown
relax
and get ready to play

do you have the
energy
cause i got all day

lead me where you want us to go

i'm ready and willing
let's take the road less traveled slow
because fluids are spilling right here right now

goodbye

initially i wished to booze you away
to blow the blues of your decay

my throat didn't burn much
after the heartache i expected

so i went out with another one
i fell in love all over again

i realized
you and your brain were so lame
you are the saddest of all men

young love

i fell in love a long time ago
with a lover wearing purple hair in chicago

he admired my despair
i revered his ramparts at his ear

we were so young
i'd never kissed anyone with the tongue

this one time we were both walking hand in hand
moving slowly to the king-sized bed

red blood smeared across his lips
animals in bed
but criminals in the head

would you stay if i say

would you stay if i say
or will you say nay and throw my forever away

i know it's more of a dream but don't betray
please sit in silence with me till the last day

if i could just make you understand
that you occupy most of my wonderland

will you just stay a little longer
and not become one of those goners

would you stay if i say
or will you say nay and throw my forever away

the play

when our kids are all grown up our hair is gray
and life turns into a retirement holiday

i will still love you
probably even more
because we will be dancing merrily in an old fashioned way

you melt my heart so much that i never want to leave
how do you always make me feel alive and take my breath away
i can't fall asleep for i want you next to me babe

breathing onto my back and embracing me every day
maybe we will sleep and wake up to each other
intoxicated with love and trying to shove ourselves back
together

it's only a dream under the stars
but do you remember
the times we fooled each other in love so tenderly
last september

a quick lipstick

love of every kind is my favorite
love of every kind catches my heart beating

the moon shines rainbow smiles and stars are bright
the sweetest feelings fight the gloom when right

i want to chug down cosmos and
get drenched in delight all the time

the red lipstick is my favorite thing
as i can always hide under its bohemian bling

addiction

addiction is a complete mess
there is nothing fair about it
just like you in moonlight

you are my flower and i am your petal
to yourself you might feel like rain
but trust me you are 'worth the pain'

you shine the brightest my love in the luminous lights
i promise i will be with you in your darkest nights

you make me happy in every way
you are the chance i am willing to chase

passing love

i was the refuge i forgot
i didn't know you are not done with your past
so sorry
we couldn't last

call me later

whenever you say goodbye
i gear up and wait
for your next lie

i want you to fly so high
that you begin to wonder
where in the picture was ever i

are you done?

there was always love
so much love
so much more love than we could ever even imagine
between hello and goodbye

i remember you clearly but i should stop now
i want to be done with you once and for all
but tell me you aren't done with me yet
are you

architecture at its best

his mom once said my smile was perfect
thank god the sheets in his bedroom were still unchecked

a piece of lingerie arched on his chair still hung there erect
his mother could have objected
then she said my smile was perfect

she was an architect of my murder
but then again too hard to detect on radar

dirty fingernails

there was a time when you would
create a fuss over my nails
nagged me to scrape the dirt trail
shape and paint the town red without fail

that was a long time ago
back when you were still in my life

i am pleased
there is no void in your absence
since i've cut you off with a kitchen knife

in my dream

between my arms you soundly sleep
no flowery dreams that we lovers can keep

while all night i look at you snoring
those tender sounds make me pour love all over you
looking at you makes me sense all your sorrows

the bounteous silken hair and ashen arms
the shapely neck and round rising breast
and all the splendours that supinely rest
between your sheets is the only time
i find my peace

to future

i was his future and happily ever after
then the rest was all a blur

everybody told me to leave
then i couldn't do it ever

bruises and cuts can disappear
wounds in the heart can never expire

silent treatment

what's the point of the silent treatment
when they don't even give a fuck about your judgment

i thought we could reach an agreement
but your rad behavior pattern has been too frequent

damn it
you don't even have any valid reason
looking down at me and giving me the cold shoulder
will not work today

i have grown a spine to push you away
to this day you think i will obey

oh my dear get your grumbling growls out of my way
please don't stay
my day is so much better when you go astray

vessel

i didn't know the vessel was leaking
when i was pouring
i didn't have a scoring

i won't live by your word
i stand here alone with broken trust
and thrown away like dirt

fyi the vessel is a metaphor for trust

what's up

she really did hurt my feelings
i still loved talking to her with hurt feelings

am i spineless and awkward
who cares

let's text her
hey what's up
my beautiful ex

पटाखा
टोटा
बम्ब
आइटम
माँ
माल
बहन
बेटी
पत्नी